© Mike Minehan

GJERTRUD SCHNACKENBERG

HEAVENLY QUESTIONS

Gjertrud Schnackenberg was born in Tacoma, Washington, in 1953. *The Throne of Labdacus* (FSG, 2000) received the Los Angeles Times Book Prize in Poetry.

ALSO BY GJERTRUD SCHNACKENBERG

Portraits and Elegies (1982)

The Lamplit Answer (1985)

A Gilded Lapse of Time (1992)

The Throne of Labdacus (2000)

Supernatural Love: Poems 1976–1992 (2000)

HEAVENLY QUESTIONS

HEAVENLY QUESTIONS

GJERTRUD SCHNACKENBERG

FARRAR, STRAUS AND GIROUX

NEW YORK

Farrar, Straus and Giroux
18 West 18th Street, New York 10011

Published in 2010 by Farrar, Straus and Giroux
First paperback edition, 2011

"Sublimaze" was originally published in *Harper's Magazine*.

The Library of Congress has cataloged the hardcover edition as follows:
Schnackenberg, Gjertrud.
    Heavenly questions / Gjertrud Schnackenberg. — 1st ed.
        p.   cm.
    ISBN 978-0-374-28307-0 (alk. paper)
    I. Title

PS3569.C5178H43 2010
811'.54—dc22

                                                2010005675

Paperback ISBN: 978-0-374-53304-5

Designed by Jonathan D. Lippincott

www.fsgbooks.com

For its generous support in the fall of 2004, the author gratefully
acknowledges the American Academy in Berlin.

NOTE

Usually translated into English as *Heavenly Questions*, the ancient poem *Tianwen* by Qu Yuan (c. 340–278 B.C.E.) is a series of unanswerable cosmological, philosophical, and mythological questions which, according to a legend from the second century C.E., the banished poet wrote on the walls of temples during his wanderings.

I am indebted to Cyril Mango's *Hagia Sophia: A Vision for Empires* (Ertuğ and Kocabıyık, 1997) for two legends about the building: an ancient legend that the Imperial Door was made of wood from Noah's ark; and a seventeenth-century Turkish legend that the hundreds of doors of Hagia Sophia could not be accurately counted because they lay under a magic spell.

Although the poem "Bedtime *Mahabharata*" departs substantially from the Sanskrit epic, I have drawn upon William Buck's one-volume reimagining of the *Mahabharata* (University of California, 1973), and upon translations of the *Bhagavad Gītā* by Juan Mascaro (Penguin, 1962) and J.A.B. Buitenen (University of Chicago, 1981).

CONTENTS

ARCHIMEDES LULLABY   3

SUBLIMAZE   9

VENUS VELVET NO. 2   25

FUSITURRICULA LULLABY   37

THE LIGHT-GRAY SOIL   43

BEDTIME *MAHABHARATA*   49

HEAVENLY QUESTIONS

ARCHIMEDES LULLABY

A visit to the shores of lullabies,
Where Archimedes, counting grains of sand,
Is seated in his half-filled universe
And sorting out the grains by shape and size.
Above his head a water-ceiling sways,
Beneath his feet the ancient magma-flows
Of metamorphic, underearth plateaus
Are moving in slow motion, all in play,
And all is give-and-take, all comes and goes,
And hush now, all is well now, close your eyes,

Distant ocean-engines pulverize
Their underwater mountains, coarse to fine,
In granite-crumbs and flakes of mica gold
And particles of ancient olivine;
And water waves sweep back and forth again,
Materialize, and dematerialize,
Retrieving counted grains and dropping more
Uncounted grains in heaps along a shore
Of granite-particled infinities,
Amassing shores for drawing diagrams.

Behind him, on the shores of Sicily,
His legendary works accumulate:
Discarded toys, forgotten thought-machines,
And wonder-works, dismantled on the sand:

A ship, reduced to ashes by a mirror;
A planetarium in hammered bronze
Whose heaven rotates, taking its own measure;
The fragment of a marble monument—
A sphere inscribed within a cylinder—
Forgotten, overgrown with stems and leaves;

A vessel, filled with water to the brim
To weigh Hiero's golden diadem,
But emptied on its side now, overturned;

And numbers fading in papyrus scrolls
He sent by ship to Alexandria:
Approximated ratios glimpsed within
The wondrously unlocked *square root of 3*;
And *3.141* . . . : a treasure-store
Marcellus cannot plunder; cannot use;
And *1.618* . . . : the weightless gold
No scales are needed for, no lock and key,
Ratio divine, untouchable in war;

And block-and-tackle pulleys; water-screws
And other spirals, angles, cubes, and spheres;
The iron lever rusting at his feet

A relic from the time he told the King
Assembled with the court: *Give me a place*
Whereon to stand, and I will move the earth;
And as he spoke, another earth appeared,
One grain among innumerable grains
And nearly weightless as a grain of sand,

And high above the giant fortress walls
Of Syracuse his mental catapults
Are hurling mental boulders one by one
At Roman warships sinking in the bay—
Far off, a shipwreck; up close, bubble foam
Sweeps forward on the sand, sweeps off again
With remnants of a Roman war machine—

Even the Roman sailors, disembarked
From sinking ships, and rowing toward the beach
In lifeboats set afloat from battleships
Now sinking in the distance—even they
Are falling fast asleep above their oars,

And undulating ropes lash in the wakes
And bob along, the ropes asleep as well—
All drifting past the legendary shores
Where Archimedes counts the grains of sand . . .

It never ends, this dire need to know,
This need to see a diagram unfold
In silent angles, drawing in the sand,

This need to see a diagram achieve
Self-organizing equilibrium
Among the mica flakes and granite-crumbs,
This need to fill the universe with sand,
And all in play, with everything in play,

And every night before he falls asleep
In cold and heavy sand, he leans to brush
The clinging sand-grains from his naked feet

And myriads appear, self-multiply,
And multiply again: Let this be X,
Let this be X times X, and let there be
More myriads of zeroes grain by grain
In sacks of sand where one by one by one
More sacks of sand are filled with other grains,
Let numbers coalesce and re-emerge
Unharmed by coalescence and unchanged;
And always let a higher number form
And every single number have a name:

Ten to the power of the sixty-third;
A *vigintillion* grains of sand, times eight;
Eight *vigintillion*, plus or minus one:
A number for the demiurge to ponder,
Sprawling in his sleep among the bags
Of sand grains pouring into Syracuse
Where Archimedes draws a diagram . . .

It never ends, this dire need to know,
Even beneath the smoking sword of war
A Roman soldier raises overhead
Mid-thought, mid-diagram, even before
He finishes the drawing at his feet,
Even before he has the chance to say:
Let whosoever can, complete—but then

A soldier lifts the smoking sword of war,
And he's forgotten what he meant to say.
Black heavens, pouring into Syracuse
In granite-particled infinities
Amass another shoreline at his feet.
He falls asleep in cold and heavy sand
And finishes his drawing in his sleep
Before the edges of the lines he drew
Begin to crumble grain by grain by grain
With everything in play, and all in play

A myriad appears; self-multiplies;
And waves of water sweep around and through,
Retrieving counted grains and dropping more
Uncounted grains in heaps in lullabies
Where Archimedes falls asleep and sees

A grain of sand appear: the final grain;
Ten to the power of the sixty-third,
Times eight; the sum complete before his eyes;
And then another grain is added: *One*;

A sack of sand tips over, pours away,
Black heavens pouring out infinities
Of sleeping islands, sleeping Sicilies,

And water waves appear and sweep away
Forgotten wonder-works and thought-machines,
And heaven revolves, a planetarium
For calculating distances between
The heavenly stars and measuring their size,
All twirling in slow motion, slower still,
And slower still, and all is sleep and peace,
The universe asleep before his eyes
Beside an ocean moving in its sleep,

And distant ocean-engines pulverize
Their underwater mountains, coarse to fine,
And water waves appear and disappear
Retrieving counted grains and leaving more
Uncounted grains in heaps in lullabies,
Where Archimedes, counting grains of sand,
Is seated in his half-filled universe,
And sorting out the grains by shape and size,
And all is well now, hush now, close your eyes,
And one . . . by one . . . by one . . . by one . . . by one . . .
The flakes of mica gold and granite-crumbs
Materialize, and dematerialize.

SUBLIMAZE

The door I crazed with knocking reappeared.
A transitory door, lit on the wall,
Drenched radiant orange, ablaze beyond the bed,
A milli-millimeter depth of red,
Painted in a nearby universe.
The soft gray afternoon lay muffled, hushed,
Dark heaven hidden behind. A nurse
Materialized, and dematerialized.
The sunset sank its heat into the wall.

I sat beside him, dozing in my coat,
Our hands entwined, my chin sunk to my chest,
A sentinel, my vigil overcome,
The password lost, a ring of useless keys
Had fallen from my hand, but never mind,
Those keys were melted down from other locks
And locks from other keys, fifth surgery
Of five, the final one I argued for
Though one by one the locks were bolted shut—
A sentinel, my vigil overcome,
But where, and to what end, and guarding what—

A sunset-painted door, with long-lost keys
Left hanging in a conjured iron ring
With blowing ribbons just this moment blown,
And drops of opiates, threefold, fourfold, five:
Door to the house where no one ever died,
With countless rings of keys in iron locks
And bolts that multiplied and multiplied—

My vigil overcome, but starting here,
I reasoned that if someone swept a hand
And all the locks fell open all at once,
And if the door fell open, he would live—
A miracle for us. Another chance.
Beloved body's beauty, lying still,
His intima, held still; narcotic trance,

We slept beside a sunset-painted door,
Crumpled beside a wall of cinder blocks.
The wall was tilting in a floor of sand,
The *Heavenly Questions* raving on the wall
Were half-dissolved, were mere graffiti now,
Though all those being-riddles lay unsolved,
Erased, then reappearing. Re-erased.

Unbidden universe, what summons us,
Awakening, unbidden, in its midst?
Unpremeditated, and unsought,
A deed without a doer doing this,
An act without a "pre-existing I";

Self-fabricating atoms, like a thought
That pre-exists the mind where it appears:
Why this—i.e., existence—why exist?
The universe is self-created where?
The universe is self-created why?

All questions put aside, perhaps for good,
Questions, O monks, that lead not to salvation.
I turned my back on heaven once and for all,
No questions anymore. Just say he'll live.
Bright doors exploded open, closed; O.R.—
Illusory door, but with a real door
Set into it, but both doors bolted shut;
But bolted shut the same as left ajar—

Enchanted knife that didn't even hurt,
Though somewhere else it seems a shadow-knife
Was cutting shadow-flesh, but never mind;
Handleless, the knife without a blade,
Said Lichtenberg; and no one could have known,
And sutures sewn with no one there to sew them,
Yet one by one in perfect order sewn
The way that seashell sutures come to be
In painless silence; painless, utterly;
Across a floor of sand we can't say where,

The speechless needle buried in the vein.
Above, a water-ceiling self-divides.
A scissors cutting through a water-surface;

Surface reflections shudder; self-repair;
Nausea; a bleaching coral reef;

Opiates. The ship of Theseus
Passing above. A water-ceiling sways.
The masts broken, torn down, no one aboard.
And bumping quietly against a reef,
Wave-dismantled, bobbing plank by plank,
Touching a shore; disintegration; foam—

The demiurge that forged the nucleus
Had set an injured molecule aside
That broke away midstream, autonomous,
And copied out its secret injury.
A break-site underwent a subtle change,
A hidden break-site in a chromosome;
A break, without apparent consequence,
And no one knew. And no one could have known.
Something smaller than a grain of sand.
But every crumb of matter in Creation
Casts a shadow, every grain of dust;
And every weightless shadow gathers mass,
Though infinitely smaller than a grain;
The speechless needle buried in the vein;
God in the distance lifting up the stone
That even God can't lift: the nucleus
In micro-desolate eternity.

Awakened briefly in a frigid room.
A blue god standing by, blue mask and gown,
Blue gloves, and dazzling waterlights and darks;
A buried memory-surge: a god's blue hand
Gestured above the opened body's rim:

All that could be done has now been done.
I am the same to all, Lord Krishna said.
To all beings, my love is ever one.

Then we two, reunited and marooned.
A door drenched radiant orange beyond the bed
Appearing in a wall of cinder blocks
Lit dimly gray. Then gone. And evening came
And took the door, frame, handles, latches, locks,
Even the black cube buried in the frame
With chisel marks around the mortise box;
Then took the wall away,

                              but all was well,
Mysterious rudiments of our farewell:
Unguarded hope's covalent bonds entwined
With opiates' covalent molecules,
A paradox inside a paradox
Of fathomless repose, the selfsame dream
That all was well, and we were going home;
But first it was imperative to find
The house where no beloved ever died,
And when you find it I'll restore his life—

We slept beside a bleaching coral reef,
The walls around us, creaking, to and fro,
And leaking light, bright water streaming through
From ceiling-lit fluorescence in the hall—
Receding planes, and looming gray-lit rooms
And coral vaults how many stories high,
A rainswept mosque anchored by semi-domes,
A distant crown of forty window-jewels,
The windows open to the elements
In transepts north and south and east and west
And rain was blowing through the vestibules
And exedrae and wings under a spell
Of doors that multiply and multiply—

A bleaching coral reef with pockmarked walls
And shining heaps of gouged-out tesserae—
Like seashell litter, slowly ground to sand,
In violet-blue, in white, in basalt green,
Vermilion, mica leaf, along the floors
Like ex-mosaics chiseled from the walls
Or future pictures still to be installed
With drops of Sublimaze. I thought he stirred;
A pockmarked coral reef, my flashlight beam
Sought out a torn mosaic's chisel-gouged,
Dismantled portrait of the panting hart
At rest, beside a stream, in Paradise:

A tongue was lapping water audibly
Behind the veil of a dreadful thirst.
My magic stag lay in a trance induced,

Driven to panting foam and scrambling
His legs to try to lift his head to drink.
I scrambled to my feet and swayed, perplexed.
Beloved body's beauty, lying still;
I pressed an ice-soaked sponge against his lips.
He thanked me, even then. *Oh say not so.*

I thought I stood beside his crumpled form
Holding an arrow broken from his side.
My fingers touched the dressing of his wound,
A shaking fever, streaming flanks; I thought
I held a broken arrow, petrified.

There was an arrow nothing could remove.
A parable crumbled along a binding.
Don't send to know, if you've been arrow-struck,
Whether the arrow's made of gold or wood;
If made of gold, extracted from what mine;
If made of wood, what kind, what tree, what grove;
Don't send to know the archer's name or age
Or occupation, place of origin,
Or whether poison soaked the arrowhead
And if it did, what antidotes are used;
Don't send to know if you were struck by chance,
Or if the arrowhead was meant for you;
It doesn't matter now; don't send to know—

Footsteps, a curtain swept aside, a nurse,
A wave of reassurances: he's fine;
What needed tending to was tended to,

And all that could be done has now been done,
And all is well and nothing left to do.
All is well and hush and never mind.

Beloved body's beauty, lying still,
His hand, silk to my lips, no questions now,
Just say he'll live. *My bluest veins to kiss,*
Said Cleopatra, holding out her hand,
If only you will tell me he will live—
And felt myself subsiding in my chair,

The puzzle solved: sunset, a rainswept mosque
In Istanbul, the legend of its doors
That lay under a spell such that no one
Could count them all, however carefully
The tally's kept—*two hundred ninety-nine,*
Three hundred doors, three hundred doors and one—
But always one was added to the sum,
Another door was always added: one

Among the doors that lay under a spell:
Some scraped the floors, with dark-rubbed radii
On marble thresholds, tilting underneath
The distant dome's transferred weight-bearing load;
And some fell open; some were spurious doors,
With curious, rusting keys in rusting locks,
Whose painted marble panels, washed away
By centuries of rain, were nonetheless
Still set in quarried marble jambs with veins

Indelible, however far and deep
Rain-pelted marble surfaces erode—

And some, torn from their ancient hinges, leaned
Against the walls in upper galleries
With chisel marks where vanished bronze was pried,
Transported from the house where no one died,
Perhaps; a miracle, another chance,
The final surgery I argued for—
Fifth surgery of five, at my request,

And some were rubble-filled and nailed shut
And plastered over: ghost doors showing through,
High up, on second-story walls, midair,
Implying long-demolished balconies.
Illusory above them, lasting scars,
Where other portals, partially begun
In unrecorded times, left incomplete,
Were hidden under black partitions hung
Like drapes, neglected, shredding on their rings—
Black curtains drawn across unbidden thoughts—

And dead-end galleries ahead were sealed
With glowing metal doors that smelled of smoke
With massive knobs in bronze, too hot to touch,
Even for dreamers' hands; behind the doors,
Ashes in heaps, still pulsing scarlet-orange.
And crumbling from its hinges, up ahead,

The oldest door, built from a cedar plank
Retrieved from Noah's ark and silver-sheathed
But shrunken, only wide enough for one.
I drew him to my chest and carried him,
We stood together at the ancient door:

Among the doors that lay under a spell,
Another door appeared: three hundred doors;
Three hundred doors and one; three hundred two—
I reasoned that if someone swept a hand
And all the locks fell open all at once
And all the doors fell open, he would live;

And ran my palm across the phantom wood—
But phantom slivers lodging in my palm
Were stabbing me awake: futility
Of every bolt and lock and handle tried.
And all that could be done had now been done.
First find the house where no beloved died
In any generation; none, I say;
No father, mother, husband, wife, or child,
No father's father, mother's mother . . . none;
But if you cannot find it, lay him down;
Lay his body down, and come away—

Covalent molecules of Sublimaze
And other alkaloids and analogues
Took down the wall in which the door I crazed
With knocking reappeared; but in his sleep;

And every seven seconds oxygen
Would slide away, exhaled, and opiates
Broke down the walls in scattered cinder blocks
We slept crumpled beside, but left a door
Still standing, bolted shut where nothing was.

Immobilized, my chin sunk to my chest,
The puzzle solved: a sunset-painted door
That came and went among the galleries—
But then another door was added: one:

Outside in the fluorescent corridor
The elevator doors slid open, closed:
A sudden opening in a concrete wall,
The elevator shaft a hollow tower
Built in the negative. Abolished space
Where bells swept up and past, plunged past and down.
A bell had broken from its rope and fell
From floor to floor to floor, descending toward
A hidden basement room, an unmarked door,
A frigid theater for Anatomy—
But no one knew, and no one could have known—

I felt the opiates touch his bluest veins:
At one a.m., at two a.m., the hour
The weightless, phantom images inside
Another's mind dissolve inside one's own:

The apparition of the body scan,
A momentary fabric, seraph-hung,
Across a momentary scaffolding.
One and the Many. Many and the One.

The apparition of the body scan,
An apparition from Vesalius,
The *Fifth Book of Anatomy*, laid bare:
Beloved body, lit in blacks and grays,
Black-soaked, and streaming in eternity,
The resurrected cavity of Galen,
In anti-particles. In gamma rays.
A visionary study of the veins,
Merely a blurry shadow on a scan;
And overhead a surgeon turns a page:

Black curtains sewn from bolts of consciousness
Are held aside by seraphs in black corners:
A stream of flowing atoms, held aside.
The presentation of a hidden sight:
Anatomy, which means the "cutting open,"
From atoms, meaning the "uncuttables,"
The indivisibles, the *Fabrica*,
The template of the "pre-existing I"—
Intangible, the fabric tourniquets
The seraphs tie and tie with anxious hands—
But when they turn, to see it for themselves,
Atoms unbind, down to their nuclei:

The mortal body, spectral to the core.
An image no one made, or made by God,
Or self-made, self-dissolving, self-aware.
Who then, or what, hallucinated this?
The tragedy of being only this,
Aristotle's *thisness*, nothing more

Among the crowds thronging the frontispiece:
The Renaissance physicians, crowding near,
Distinguished faculty, apprentices,
Ambassadors, and workmen of the trades,
Students of medicine, nobility,
And clerks of law and church—and all alone,
Above the throng, a rearing skeleton—
And some sway on their feet, some hold their own,
Some turn away, some snuffed out at the sight:

A table, heaped with tools of the trade:
The cutting table, instruments arrayed;
The knife of the anatomist, beheld:
An iron scale sinks: the heart is weighed—

And standing in the foreground undisturbed,
Philosophers, who weigh hallucinations,
Are questioning students of medicine:
What is the largest object in Creation?
The Whole of wholes, Ein Sof, *Totality?*
What can't be stood outside of, looking on?
What is the all in all in all in All?

And its circumference?—the brain is weighed
Without its weightless, phantom images—

Anaesthesia's curtain briefly lifts:
A chaos-surge: a frigid basement room
Without locality, and massless, drifts—

A distant vacuum cleaner vacuuming
The surface of an undiscovered moon,
Perplexia, revolving upside down,
Orbit-knocked, but holding to its path

Above our room, above another earth,
Where other moons are tugging other seas;
Black troughs, white crests, black troughs, directionless
Successive walls collapsing, every wave
Torn down by its own foaming edge that pulls
White fringes down from transitory walls—

Water divides-repairs, before-behind;
And churning pre- and post-chronology
Where everything is happening at once—
A curtain lifted, white; but falling, black:
Black sails appearing on a distant rim—

There will be other ships of Theseus,
Mirage-like, on the rims of distant gulfs,
Gliding in silence under other cliffs;
Other Aegeans, other nameless seas

Dissolving oceanic memories
In other future ocean-vanishings;
And other drowning and emerging coasts
Where long-eroded outcroppings of rock
That once upon a time were continents
Are cliffs; then jutting fragments that divide
A shoreline where an ocean opened-closed

On other, deeper mid-Atlantic rifts
Where other, higher Everests, submerged
A mile below the surface, came and went
Where other chains of mountains come and go—

And other earths with other molten cores,
Other beginnings, other long-lost ends
In other times, in other firmaments,
Before-behind;
                    A ship of Theseus
Mirage-like on a distant rim, appears,
Black troughs, white crests, black troughs, directionless—
Touching a shore; disintegration; foam . . .

Wherever sleep has taken us, we stir,
Surprised; the sunlight raging in our faces,
Recalling where we are, but both alive;
His smile igniting, happy: let's go home.
And drowsing near me, reaches for my hand.
The room alight.

Weightless prisms spill
Across the ceiling, scattered from my ring,
And quiver: multiplying, self-disclosed,
The chains of planets flow, and disappear.
Fan out. Then disappear. Fan out again.
Eternities released from snares of djinns.

"Only if a self, located in
One possible world, can synthesize itself
Long distance, in another world, to be
A nonself there . . ."

The morning nurse arrives,
All gentle comfort, asking how he feels,
And hangs a vacuum sack of liquid drugs
Above his head, and double-checks the line,
And brings fresh ice with soaking sponges fixed
To plastic wands for me to swab his lips—
And says: No sips allowed. And says that we're
Awaiting lab results, no word so far;
And scribbles notes; and says: he's doing fine.

Trembling prisms hang among her words.
Venus-Earth-and-Mars: the surgeon can't
Be here until tonight, to meet with you.
I twist my ring, and weightless prisms spill
Across the ceiling. Gathered overhead,
The planets tremble. Trembling violet-blue.
And trembling yellow-green. And trembling red.

VENUS VELVET NO. 2

My pencil, Venus Velvet No. 2,
The vein of graphite ore preoccupied
In microcrystalline eternity.
In graphite's interlinking lattices,
Symmetrically unfolding through a grid
Of pre-existent crystal hexagons.
Mirror-image planes and parallels.
Axial, infinitesimal bonds.
Self-generated. Self-geometrized.
A sound trapped in the graphite magnitudes.
Atoms, electrons, nuclei, far off.
A break, without apparent consequence.
Near-far, far-near, those microfirmaments.
Far in, the muffled noise of our goodbyes.

The surgeon, seeking only my surrender,
Has summoned me: an evening conference.
We sit together in the Quiet Room.
He cannot ask for what I'm meant to give.
No questions anymore. Just say he'll live.
A world of light leaks through the double doors,

Fluorescent mazes, frigid corridors,
Polished linoleum, arena sand
Where hope is put to death and life is lost
And elevator doors slide open, closed.
The towers of the teaching hospital.
The field where death *his conquering banner shook.*

My writing tablet, opened on the table.
I touch it with my hand. The paper thins.
The paper's interwoven filaments
Are bluish gray and beige. No questions now.
What is the chiefest deed that's asked of us.
No questions anymore. No questions now.
I turned my back on heaven for good, but saw
A banner shaken out from heaven's walls
With apparitions from Vesalius:
A woodcut surgeon opening a book
Of workshop woodcuts, skilled, anonymous,
The chisel blade of the engraver felt
Reverberating through the wooden blocks
Among eroded words, ornately carved:
Annihilation, subtly engraved:
All those whom lamentation cannot save
Grown fainter through successive folios.
A seraph turns a page above: he'll live;
Then turns a page again: he can't survive.
I turn the page myself, and write: he'll live.
Smell of my sweat embedded in my clothes.

The surgeon says: we've talked with him; he knows.
A seraph leaning near, *Oh say not so.*
Not so. Not so. My wonder-wounded hearer,
Facing extinction in a mental mirror.
A brilliant ceiling, someone's hand on his.
All labor, effort, sacrifice, recede.
And then: I'm sorry. Such a man he is.

Visionary crystallography.
Electron noise brimming in pencil lead.
A sound trapped in the graphite magnitudes.
Far in, the muffled noise of our goodbyes
In self-repeating crystal symmetries
As graphite self-destructs in shearing off
Abraded words and microcrystals break
In microscopic heaps of graphite dust:
My pencil, scribbling, giving up on us:

A pinpoint leak of blood that can't be traced.
A mass embedded underneath the heart.
Hepatic portal vein that routes the blood
Throughout the tract of the intestine maze
And soaks the liver's capillary beds.
The intima. A bleeding deep inside.
Something smaller than a grain of sand.
Mechanisms poorly understood.
All that could be done has now been done.
I write the words, with vitals liquefied.

A page is turned above: it did no good.
A page is turned again: it did no good.
Then fingers touch a page that can't be turned.

But if it did no good, then how could I
Have watched as toxins dripped how many times
Into his bluest veins from hanging tubes
With hypodermic fangs, and how could he
Have offered up his veins without a word,
Except to reassure me it's all right
And never lose his confidence and wait
Throughout how many closed eternities,
Like Theseus bound to a chair with snakes.
The ship of Theseus passing overhead.
Our hands entwined: a single heart drained white.
And all that could be done has now been done
And I sat by. Seat of oblivion.
And saw, behind the hypodermic fangs,
The long pink throats of snakes, and sat chairbound,
And spellbound, and heartbound, and cobra-struck,
Though for his sake I would have risen up
To crush the jaws of snakes with my bare hands.

The tablet paper, thinning at my touch.
—He said of you, Nothing can conquer her.—
The words appear, the pencil unaware
Of what it writes: *But you did know how much,*
Words of defeated Antony, when all
Was lost, in graphite's faded gray: *But you
Did know how much you were my conqueror.*

The tablet paper, bluish gray and beige.
The graphite pressed and bound with binding clay.
Graphite, a non-magnetic mineral.
Yet magnets hold the phrases to the page.

A brilliant ceiling light, the god's blue glove,
The gesture at the opened body's rim:
All that could be done has now been done.
One and the Many. Many and the One.

How could I turn and say: but this is him.
How could I say: he bounded when he walked.
How could I say: when he came home at night,
A gust of snowy air around his coat,
I drew him closer, holding his lapels;
He caught me by the wrists and closed his eyes.

How could I say I tried to memorize
The truthful face, his smile a truthful blaze
Untrammeled still. I tried to learn by heart
The light-brown gaze: unguarded chrysolite
From such another world that heaven made.
Left iris, with a comet-fleck of gold.
How could I memorize his gentle ways.
The way he mingled friendliness with passion,
Plain dealing, open-handed, unafraid.
The swift, reflexive generosity.

His striking conversation, magic ease
In seeking what the other could, then more,
In understanding, warmly understood;
A quest for truth but not for certainty.

And the integrity I idolized:
Another's mystery never trifled with.
No one was belittled in those eyes.

Nothing denied, held back, or kept apart.
And never lost his gentle ways with me.
And wanted power over no one else,
But master of his heart, and of himself,
A mind that never darkened, mastermind,
Fountain of pulsing energy at play,
Unshackled, unentangled, unconfined.

Beneath the reading light, his pillowed head
A crimson-outlined silhouette at night,
His profile marble-carved, noble, sun-warmed,
Even at night, in winter, ruddy-tinged.
Red-gold of Titian's pigment-laden brush.

The red-lit aureate curving of his ear,
Warm-blooded velvet, made for lips to find.
I kissed his brow good night and felt the touch
Of lashes brush my chin before they closed.
Untroubled love. Unmarred. And quiet sleep,

His head a silken weight against my chest,
Velvet inner elbow, dangled foot,
Voluptuous surrender, unarmed Mars,
Even in sleep, composed. Even in sleep
Possessive of my hand. Still self-possessed.

Never again our idyll-nights of peace,
Never again to have him to myself.
White sheets, white blanket shadows, whitest rest,

His sleeping hand beneath the reading light
Abandoning an ancient paperback
Of Buddhist parables that fell away
When I retrieved it, dropping page by page:

Oh say not so, Ananda, say not so,
Buddha replied, when his pupil-companion
Came to him, and sat down on one side,
And set aside his begging bowl, and said,
"My teacher, isn't beauty half the goal?
For doesn't half the holy life consist
Of drawing near to beauty, step by step?"
Oh say not so, Ananda, say not so;
Not half, he answered. *Say it is the whole.*

My pencil point, hallucinating scrolls,
Scrolling and unscrolling on the page.
A wind was pushing shapes through waves of water,
But whether shapes of water or of wind,

Impossible to say: unscrolling waves
In slow velocities and solitudes

Unwheeling in volutes and streaming spheres
And transitory sets of spiral stairs
That climb-descend themselves, and disappear
On wheeling waterwheels in waterwheels,
Expending wave-momentum piling up

Black waves in heaps, then turning oceans white;
Black troughs, white crests, black troughs, directionless
But pulling back, then pushing east to west
And west to east, black troughs, directionless,
Endings accumulating endlessly
And gathering accumulated force
How many thousand miles, and all to press

Ahead, but to what end, all for the sake
Of using oceanic force to lay
A fringe of foam along a passing crest,
Then pulling foam down transitory walls
And pushing walls ahead, and all to break
In momentary peaks along a shore
We can't say where, and briefly taking back
What's briefly given, everything in play,
In gulfs that close and open; close again;

And waves of water pushing shapes through wind,
And each the other's mine, no gulfs to cross
But crossing gulfs in turn, and historyless—

How could I say we wanted nothing else
And nothing less and nothing more than this,
To find each other's spirit's melting point
And changing states, never such nakedness
Between such two, *my bluest veins to kiss*,
Never such certainty, the selfsame quest

Not to possess, but to be known; to know;
Not needing it confirmed; confirming it.
And in a place arrived at on our knees,
He tugged my face to his, as if he took
His own life in his hands; all gentle ways;
A lifelong quest for you; and won't let go
Unless you leave your fingerprints on me;
A gaze returned, the softest counterblow;

And gathering my hair in gentle fists,
Persuasion's force with no one to persuade,
Only persuading hairpins from my hair,
Their falling on the floor, a plunder-gift;

And nothing lost, but found and found again;
And not conquest, but everything in play
Given, not taken; taken anyway,
And not to keep in any case; but kept;
Possessed, but not in order to possess;
Selfsame, self-owned, self-given, self-possessed,
And all in play. But conquered nonetheless.

The yellow maze of frigid corridors
Shone black; it didn't matter where; I left,
But sightless, pulling on my winter coat,
My boots pulled over sweatpants, hat and gloves
Pulled on, indoors; as if to take him home;

A maze of concrete blocks, and doors in rows
In halls and hallways swallowing the rooms
And blind corners that swallowed up the halls
And elevator doors slid open, closed
On hollow towers built in the negative
Where bells, plunged from their ropes, were falling past.
A crust of unshed tears above my throat.
Give him back. Tell me what I can give.
Without an altar, death. Without a place
To pray. To beg for life. But let him live.

I found a phone booth, place to bawl unheard,
And sank beneath its automatic light.
The phone book hanging from a broken chain—
I drew it to my lap, a sprawling weight
Of paper pulp from long-forgotten trees
Snuffed-out and boiled down and pressed in sheets
Of ashen paper, faintly blue and gray,
A book unreadable and authorless,
A mystical directory of the living,
Each page a random sample of Creation
And changing version of the Book of Life;
I ran my glove over the listings: throngs;

And found his name, still listed with the living,
Whose stories vanish, leaving only names
Recycled and reused. This faring on
And on, O mendicants. And overhead

A page that can't be turned. He can't survive.
But let him live. My gloves pressing my eyes,
A thousand stars rotating inwardly
A millimeter past the streamered dark,
And nameless comet-phosphenes streaking by.
Without an altar, death. Without a place.

Hanging in mirror-black, lit from above,
My frightened face, kneaded in violet wax.
My face, hanging above my lap, streamed out.
I tried to press it back with clumsy gloves.

FUSITURRICULA LULLABY

A visit to the shores of lullabies,
So far from here, so very far away,
A floor of sand, it doesn't matter where,
And overhead a water-ceiling sways;
A shell is summoned to materialize—
The holy life, a spiral, hushed and pure,
Complete unto itself—a spiral shell
Is summoned from a substratum of wonder:
And all is well now, hush now, close your eyes,
Around a primal, ragged nucleus
Accumulated layers crystallize:

An embryonic seashell pulls itself
Through being-portals intricately placed
In seas of non-existence; caught; self-caught
In nets of pasts-and-futures synchronized
In present-nows: the Many and the One—

It doesn't matter, really, how it's done,
The how of it; the why; it doesn't know
How atoms in the ancient paradox
Can pass from *unseen particles* to *seen*

Or why a chain of atoms interlocks
And manifests in blurry pink and green;
It doesn't matter really, where it's from—
Descended from an ancient nacre-dream,
Self-fabricating through genetic codes
Without an archetype to utilize,
As if the wondrous deed it's summoned to
Were all that ever mattered, seam by seam
Volutions from a nacre-nucleus
Of violet iridescence: being-whorl
With everything in play, and all in play,
And all is well now, hush now, close your eyes—

A shell appears—*Fusiturricula*—
And uses its inherited clairvoyance
To plot a logarithmic spiral round
An axis of rotation evermore
And evermore-forevermore unseen,
Through pre-existing numbers, *one-two-three*,

And shyly browsing algae as it ponders
Angular momentum; symmetry;
Successively self-generating curves
Projecting helixes, the axis fixed;
Then tilting on its axis; torsion-tilt;
Compulsion and desire mixed with toil;
An overhanging cusp becomes a spire
By pushing up and forward on the coil:

Irregularly oscillating whorls
Are flaring out in ruffled calcium;

Pure *rhythmia*;
            Slow motion suturings,
With no one there to sew them, perforate
The apex, boring through: a water-vent,
Inhalant and exhalant;
                       knotted threads
Are pulled to fasten equidistant nodes
Along a helix-rim;
               a clockwise twist
And twirling stripes through interrupted bands
Are darkly lit, through brilliant whites and creams,
Like lightning bolts in violet-tinted brown
That zigzag in slow motion, down and down
From node to node to node; a lightning dream
Descending ridge by ridge:
                    Sensation: *Fizz*—
Salt water circulating past and through
The ruffled aperture—existence is
A taste of ocean water on a tongue—

And then *Fusiturricula*, intent
On browsing, sets in motion moving veils
Of sands that long ago and far away
Were magma rocks with twisted veins of ore
From which the sand was ground and empty shells
Like lightning-stricken spires, surface-fused
With used-up bolts of lightning, lie around—

Nacreous, in almost-silence, hushed
Among the lulling engines of the sea—

But hush now, close your eyes now, all is well:
Underwater ink enlarges, blurs,
In violet-brown across a spiral shell:
A record of volutions fills a scroll
With wondrous deeds and great accomplishings,
A record of a summons not refused:

Of logarithms visible and fused
With thoughts in rows of spiral beaded cords
As X goes to infinity; impearled;
Violet; and inviolate; self-endowed;

Itself the writing, and itself the scroll
The writing's written on; and self-aware
With never-ever-to-be-verbalized
Awareness of awareness of awareness,
Instantiation; all in play; a sole
Immaculate example of itself;

And in the aperture, the remnants of
A Heavenly Question, lightly brushed across
With opalescent ore of consciousness:
The universe is where? Is hanging where?

And overhead a water-ceiling sways,
And all is done in play; in heaven above

The ceiling of the sea is drawing streams
Of shining answers through its question-sieves:
Is matter the enchanted lathe? Or mind?
But which one spirals from the other's blade?

And all the waves at the beginning-end
Of all that comes and goes and takes and gives
And all in play and all that dies and lives
Materializes; dematerializes;
Five, and four, and three, and two, and one—
And all is brought to being; all effaced;

And all that could be done has now been done;
And all is well and hush now, never mind;
Fusiturricula slowly withdraws
Its being; self-enfolding; self-enclosed;
And all it toiled for turns out to be
No matter—nothing much—nothing at all—
Merely the realm where *"being"* was confined
And what was evanescent evanesced;

And then a spiral shell washed by a wave
Is carried forward in a foaming crest;
But that was long ago and far away,
It doesn't matter, really, when it was,
And close your eyes now, hush now, all is well,
And far from here, so very far away,

A wave sets down an empty spiral shell
And draws away, it doesn't matter where,
Among the other waves that come and go,
And other waves appear and disappear
And hush now, all is well, and far from here

All heaven and earth appear; and evanesce;
A self-engulfing spiral, ridge by ridge,
That disappears in waves that come and go
And all that could be done is done; and seven;
And six; and five; and four; and three; and two;
And one . . . and disappearing . . . far away . . .
Enraptured to the end, and all in play,
A spiral slowly turns itself in heaven.

THE LIGHT-GRAY SOIL

Shambles of grief in daylight under heaven.
I sit among the living, in a park,
Three miles from where he's laid to rest, three months.
Foot traffic dimly swirls around me, throngs
Of the unbidden pass me, the unburied.
I sit inside a coat he gave me once.
Systole and diastole. Not knowing when
I halted at this bench, not knowing when
I ceased to stalk the sidewalk, came to rest,
Not knowing, since it doesn't matter when.
My heart-walls moving of their own accord.
A helpless deed, systole and diastole,
Two halves carved from a pre-existing whole.
Contracting, and the chambers fill with blood.
Dilating, and the blood is surging through.
Five heaps of being, five, the beggar said.
O beggar, I have seen the mound of earth
When all the rivers call their fountains back.
I wore my shoes away, I wore away
The stockings from my feet, seeking the house
Where no beloved person ever died,

No father, mother, husband, wife, or child.
Earth's crust diminishing beneath my feet.
The mantle glimpsed. The churning, iron core.
My hand lies next to me, begging, unheld:
Another earth. Give me another earth.
Then hide my hand, ashamed I couldn't help.

                    My fingers touch
A penny, long forgotten in my coat,
Forgotten in the shock, December eighth,
Midnight emergency, a penny swept
Together with belongings from his coat
Into a sack of "Personal Effects,"
Then locked away, then given to the "Spouse."
Nearly relinquished, nearly overlooked.
Surely the last he touched, now briefly mine.
A token of our parting, blindly kept.
Alloy of zinc, the copper thinly clad,
Still ringing from the blow, blow of the die
That struck the faceless planchet long ago.
Struck in the "Kingdom of the Final Cause."
Blindly my fingers touch the edge. It thins.
Worn as if one side had disadhered.
Eroded, yet its force cannot be spent.
How many hands have worn away the image.
The frail, raised inscription of the motto
Nearly intangible within the rim.
One and the Many. Many and the One.
How could I turn and say, But this is him.

Nobody, looking at my face, can see
That I am doubling back and doubling back,
The room where breath is fought for, summoned here.
I press damp lashes shut. Catch sight of him.
Something one wants to say before one dies.
What were the words I tried to cast a spell
To understand? *Stay, stay.* His eyes seized mine,
He summoned all his strength to move his gaze
To look out at the night, a final time.
Mysterious rudiments of our farewell
The night of January twenty-third.
Never again the moon in heaven above:

Blue circular gorges, hanging overhead,
And heaven's hanging rivers gently wind
Along the rilles of lunar magma-flows,
And shadow massifs, scattered bright debris,
Steep cliffs and winding valleys, peak by peak,
And chains of peaks extending out of sight,
Bright looming ramparts guarding empty heavens,
And lone peaks left behind in shadow bays
That overflow in every melting phase,
Engulfing comet-strikes and glancing blows
And radiating rays; and rim by rim
A silver scythe materializes, mows
The circular black floors of crater wells
In silence and slow motion to expose
An underlying wonder: brightest white
That shades to chalk and gray and blue and beige,

And watercolor lilac shadows shade
To lavender in pale, tinted bays
Flooded with water light, and lit with waves
Of lava flows whose waters vaporize
In ocean-bays where no one ever sails;
Where ultimately powder gray prevails,

Obliteration, fathomless repose;
And meteoric ages' orbit-blows
From relict lunar epochs still depict
Hallucinated maps of ancient time,
A lit-up record of the time it slowed,
Revolving in slow motion on its axis,
Ever slower, ever more, until it seemed
To halt, but didn't halt, and seemed to hold
Itself forever still in such a night,
Held in the grip of earth's magnetic hold,
In synchronous rotation with the earth,
Suspended, floodlit in eternity
The night of January twenty-third—

I held him like a passion-tattered cloak.
At four a.m., the hour when one of us
Would turn in sleep to throw a leg across
The other one, protective, unaware,
I knelt, and pressed my forehead to the sheet.
The binding cloth, uncut, undyed, unsewn,
In heaven above, but gathered in my hand.
The end prepared before the sight of all.

A nurse, touching my shoulder: he passed away.
I sought his face: the truthful countenance,

Inviolate stronghold, refuge and redoubt.
Facing extinction in a mental mirror.
The still-unbroken substratum of wonder.
The *mutual flame from hence.* The blowing out.

Forever rest. His head sunk to his chest,
As if he bowed his head at last before
The helpless deed that we were summoned to.
Forever, ever rest. His hand in mine,
Possessive of my hand. All he possessed.
And when I drew my hand away from his,
His hand lay open, certain I was there.
Let nothing evermore be dear to me.

I stood instinctively to hear the call.
The resident physician, feeling for
The artery. A witness from the staff.
Whispered consolation. Four-fifteen.
The time and date and cause recorded, signed.
I swayed, dead on my feet, among the living,
Then stood away, unbidden. Still his wife.
But couldn't draw one breath on his behalf.
Nor add a single heartbeat to his life.

A gust of damp cement blows gently near me.
I breathe the scent of rained-on concrete sidewalks,
Cold gravel, water-worn, black when it rains,
Then light-gray when it dries. I breathe the scent
The gravel has, when evening rain arrives.

O beggar, I have seen the light-gray soil.
My begging hand lies near. I've seen the end.
The body's tattered cloak. The blaze of eyes.
Something one wants to say before one dies,
Unspoken now. Give me another earth.
If heaven could offer such another one.

I stood, barefoot and powerless, and heard
The distant drum in heaven begin to beat
That takes up when a heart falls motionless.
I stood instinctively to hear the call.
Beyond the muffled noise of our goodbyes,
The bindings falling from the swaddled drum
Fall quietly. Before the sight of all,
Before the sight of each and every one,
Untouched, the immaterial knot unties.

BEDTIME MAHABHARATA

Forgotten in the shock, our chess set sprawls,
An ancient kingdom, earthquake-overturned,
Shut in the dark, behind the cabinet doors.
The sacked metropolis, the useless wars,
Fragments of battles waged when all was lost,
A war, we can't say when, we can't say where,
Two tiny armies, carved, immobilized,
Two armies, diametrically opposed,
Two mirror-image armies cast aside
And jumbled, sliding from the tilted board,
Where one by one mortals are driven off,
And square by square mortals are borne away,
And left for dead behind the cabinet doors.
Jumbled as one, the slayers and the slain,
And each to each, all wars are civil wars,
Two warring sides carved from a broken tusk,
The broken tusk from which they're carved, a god's,
Whose sacrifice still overhangs the board
Where everything that ever happened fades—

That night, when all was lost, he let his head
Sink back against the pillows; took my hand;
Our chessboard set aside forever now.
Two players, matched in wonder and resolve,
Called into other wars, and not in play,
Though all those being-riddles lay unsolved,
And asked me for a story, sinking back,
A being-riddle buried in a story.
A tale about the origins of chess.

I sat beside him, huddled toward the bed,
Annihilation gusting near; all night
A book lay open in my lap, unread—

Just as the ink was drying on the law
That *noncombatants are inviolate*,
Out of the blue, heaven-colliding wars
And mirror-image towers, moving off,
Ashes impregnated with human souls—

The battles of the *Mahabharata*
Lay faded in our ancient paperback,
Dark-yellow paper, crumbled from the binding,
Old wars scorching the page: we idled there
Together at the smoke-carved cliffs of heaven.

The hero-archer halted, hung his head,
His godly bow Gandiva drooping down,
A deadweight on his shoulder: cognizant
Of useless losses, useless vanquishings,

And having seen his enemies advance—
The mirror-image mortals drawing near
Were family members, sacred teachers, friends—
His arrows humming, on the verge of flight
Before-behind: he halted, hung his head:
This battle is not mine. I will not fight.

All night the book lay open in my lap.
A being-riddle buried in a story.
I leafed to the beginning. *Long ago*
And far away and once upon a time . . .
In such a night as this, in such a night,
With mirror-image towers moving off,
When all was lost, and nothing to be done,
Out of the blue, heaven-colliding wars—
The god of writers broke his pen in half.

The god of writers, rushing to record
The battles of the *Mahabharata,*
The onslaughts recollected blow by blow,
In reconstructed sequences of time,
Whose agony whose grievance justified,
Which squandered universals squandered lives,
And which side had possession of the board,
And who had won and lost and lost and won—
Hurriedly trying to record
The names of each and every one who died,
Mid-genealogy, mid-epitaph—
The god of writers broke his pen in half.

His pen lay useless, broken in the midst
Of "Everything That's Happened Until Now"
Prefaced by "Everything That Came Before"—
A tale about the origins of chess,
Endings accumulating endlessly,
Unending wars, beyond his broken pen:

Once upon a time, war drums aroused
Chaotic gongs, and horns wailing for war
Were summoning the pieces to the board,
And chariots in slow motion grinding past
On mammoth wheels carved with battle scenes
Were drawing toward a clutch of soldier pawns
With spears like lightning springing from the ground,
And elephants arising on all fours
With howdahs swaying, tugging on their ropes,
Were jangling their rope-strung iron bells
And brilliant banners wind-whipped on their poles
Were ringing with their streams of bell-strings high
In northern India—
                    He squeezed my hand:
What sentence was he writing when it broke?
A smile, in such a night, with weeks to live.
Pajamas fever-soaked, trying to stave
Annihilation off another night.
The gentleness that nothing could repay.
I pressed his hand's blue veins against my lips.
A bedtime story, all that we had left,
And mirror-image towers moving off.

We're never told. The story doesn't say,
It doesn't tell us where it broke, or when.
The story simply says, he broke his pen.

Perhaps it broke mid-sentence when he wrote:
Even Lord Krishna couldn't end the wars . . .
And mirror-image towers turned to smoke.

Or broke in the reverberating shock
Of war drums struck so hard the heads of drums
Exploded outward into gaping stars
And bloodstained towers dematerialized,
Ashes impregnated with human souls
Who couldn't save each other or themselves,
Their stories broken off, the fragments fused,
Strangers and neighbors, enemies and friends,
Soldiers and noncombatants: fused, alone;
The conquered and the conqueror were one;
And all that could be done had now been done,

And once upon a time, in such a night,
Just as the ink was drying on the law
That *noncombatants are inviolate*,
A postulate across all possible worlds,
A distant shock, a shock we can't say what,
A shock that jarred the cabinet doors apart,
The cabinet doors jarred open on the sight
Of mirror-image towers, moving off,

A chess set sprawled, forgotten in the shock—
A war, we can't say when, we can't say where,
Evaporated: nothing happened here,
The nameless battles surging through a maze
Had vanished; everything that happens fades;
A thousand nights of play had disappeared
As if the thousand nights had never been,
And all that could be done had now been done,
But then another night was added: one:

The black castles, upended on their squares,
Poured shadow from their djinn-carved crenellations.
The warlords at a standstill: latency:

The djinn who oversaw the Balkan Wars
Unsheathed his knife in 1369,
Idolatrously carving sets of chess
For Tamburlaine, not knowing what they're for,
And eavesdropped on the stories night by night:
What is a labyrinth of bloodless war?
Scheherazade began: *What is a maze*
Whose walls are fabricated out of air?
Towers and mosques appeared beneath his blade,
Turrets and parapets and siege-machines
With pennants fluttering; armies appeared
From cities in Scheherazade's archives—
Baghdad, Aleppo, Cairo, Samarkand—
What makes the indivisible divide?

He set the curious idols on the squares.
At once the squares were fully occupied
With forces moving of their own accord:
The Field of Blackbirds opened, all in play,

Two facing mirror-image Prince Lazars,
Seated on tiny thrones, knee-deep in pawns,
Their armies whittled down, their kingdoms carved
With cutting implements, the drums of war
Exploding outward into gaping stars—
He swept them off, and set them out again:

Two facing mirror-image Bajazets,
Prosecuting thunderbolt campaigns
Through millimeter lines drawn up between
What was foreseeable and what foreseen,
The squares like iron cages welded shut—
He swept them off again, and set them out:

Two facing mirror-image Tamburlaines,
Whose bone-carved dynasties, superimposed
On boards with extra squares, extended from
The pass where Mings had locked the Gate of Jade
To counter-realms where little sultan-kings,
Wrist-bound and ankle-bound with knots entwined
On ropes that he could pull from Samarkand,
Were forced to shuffle, yanked from side to side,
East-west, before-behind—

redoubled now,
Blindfolded fury willed another pawn
To move, with all in play, all fury blind,

And bloodstained towers dematerialized
Like black castles, upended on the squares,
Scheherazade, mid-tale: *In such a night,*
When eighty thousand troops of Genghis Khan
Had finished their besieging of Herat,
Its towers tilted sideways on the ground.
Only forty inhabitants survived—
Forty, from a million trembling souls.
The victors galloped east.

What is a maze
Whose walls no one has ever touched or seen,
Whose walls are rearranged with every step,
A labyrinth whose walls are built of air
But may as well be built from quarried stone
That elephants enslaved by Tamburlaine
Were forced to drag from India and set
In moving walls in phantom battlefields—
Intangible, and yet so obdurate
No potentate can overturn or raze
Their stones or rearrange their twists and turns
To relocate the secret passageways
That guard the throne rooms where they sit exposed;
What is this immaterial labyrinth?

He stopped his knife, mid-air, mid-tale, mid-war,
Mid-massacre, mid-tournament, mid-siege:
And saw his face reflected in the blade
Where gouts of other djinns slid from the edge
And phantom pictures flickered in his brain—
The teller and the listener were one,
Creator and created, each to each,
Two players matched in wonder and resolve:

But morning came; Scheherazade withdrew;
The riddle broken off; the flames blown out;
The thousand nights blown out like candle flames
But blown out by whose lips she doesn't say,
Self-lit, perhaps, and self-extinguishing,
And stored wherever unlit flames are kept,
All vanishing, all self-creating time
Evaporated: nothing happened here
Though white smoke burgeoned from a thousand wicks;
The bloodless battles surging through a maze
Where everything that ever happened fades
Were all in play,
                        and yet his knife was red
In Persia's brilliant morning sun—he fled
To rinse his knife in mountain waterfalls
Hanging above Afghanistan, and saw,
Beyond the mountains of the Hindu Kush,
Which means *the slaughter of the infidels,*

Lord Krishna, whirling in his chariot,
Returning from his quest to end the wars—

As gaily as a grasshopper who whirls
In his green chariot, forth on summer gusts,
In brilliant sunshine, everything in play,
Lord Krishna whirled above *Himalaya*
With bell-strings streaming from his chariot poles,
Returning from his quest to end the wars,
The useless wars, the *Mahabharata*,
The tale of "All That's Happened Until Now"
Prefaced by "Everything That Came Before"—
With everything in play, and all in play,

The god of writers rushing to record
A tale about the origins of chess,
Where everything that ever happened fades,
Endings accumulating—yet his pen
Had found the end of war, caught up to all
That ever happened; all that came before;
And synchronizing all the thens-and-nows
In writing how
            Lord Krishna, sweeping down,
Returning from his quest to end the wars,
Sprang from his chariot—
                  and pealing bells
Broke from their ropes, and soldiers broke their swords,
And archers broke their arrows, elephants
Were kneeling down in wonder on the squares,

With broken tusks lowered in reverence,
And women shook their chimes in ribbon-streams,
And children swarmed and scooped the dust for joy,
The wars were at an end; but Krishna said,
Lightfooted, springing from his chariot seat,
And overjoyed to see them, but surprised:

Oh no, I couldn't bring an end to war;
I can't untie the immaterial cords
That bind us to our deeds; nobody can;
Intangible the strands that tie themselves
In transitory knots of "who" and "where"—
And then untying of their own accord—
But all that could be done has now been done.
And all is done in play, all done in play.

A gust of bells died off, dispirited.
The battles of the *Mahabharata*
Crumbled to dust across the checkered board,
The mortals shrinking back, falling away,
All driven off again, not knowing where,
Beyond the squares, between existences.
And, overhung with anguish and malaise,
The banners, shaken out in triumph, sank.
Far off, the bloodstained cries of elephants
Mourning the jumbled slayers and the slain.
What is it binds us to our deeds? What is
The sacrifice that can't be asked of us?
Unbidden universe, what summons us,
Awakening, unbidden, in its midst?

Then all those fragment-sequences in time
Swept toward a place before chronology
Where everything is happening at once
And everything that ever happened fades,
Forgotten like an unrecorded storm
That swept the earth a thousand years ago.
Ten thousand years. A hundred thousand years.
Materialized, and dematerialized:
The yugas, briefer than a lightning fork.

The hero-archer halted, hung his head,
His godly bow Gandiva drooping down,
A deadweight on his shoulder: agony
Of mirror-image mortals pressing near,
Family members, sacred teachers, friends.
Useless losses, useless vanquishings.
The arrows ready, humming, on the verge
Of flight, behind-before: implausible
That armies in slow motion craved control
Of barren, useless squares. Better to be
A beggar in the road than king of this.

He sagged beneath the deadweight of his bow,
His ancient arrows crumbling in his hand
Eroded, yet their force could not be spent:
Set these alight. My weapons should have been
Reduced to ash and cinders long ago.
This battle is not mine. I will not fight.

The cabinet doors jarred open at the shock:
A mildewed drawer in northern India.
A checkered game board, breaking at the seams,
And crumbled faces in worm-riddled wood
And chariots crumbled on their axle beams
And chunks of uncarved ivory, petrified,
And heaps of ivory shavings: untold tales
Of battles never fought and unlived lives
And useless squares for legendary wars
That never happened; deaths that no one died;
A board where ivory molecules subside.
Unborn is best of all. Unborn is best.

Lord Krishna swept his hand: bring me the board,
Bring me the immaterial labyrinth
Where everything that ever happened fades.
Bring me the knife for carving elephants
From broken ivory tusks, bring me the lathe
From which the mirror-image towers are turned.
Bring me the kings and counselors and pawns,
Bring me the conquering banner death shook out
Above the long-forgotten battlefield.
And all in play
                    he set the pieces out,
His blue hand moving quickly; latency;
He saw the indivisible divide:
Raja, and *Mantri*, *Gajah*, *Padati*.
At once the squares were fully occupied
With forces moving of their own accord,

All synchronized in present thens-and-nows:
What's won or lost when this is lost or won?
A war, we can't say where, we can't say when:
He swept them off;
                    then set them out again:

A flutter-gust of bells; war drums aroused
Chaotic gongs and horns wailing for war,
Oblivious, gong-deafened potentates
And blank-faced counselors mirrored in a maze
And pawns arrayed for shock-wave turbulence
With swords like lightning leaping from the ground,
And deed-bound archers, bell-strung elephants
Arising slowly, swaying on all fours,
The Thunderbolt Formation, lightning-flagged—
Out of the blue, heaven-colliding wars—
All summoned to the board they can't say why,
A war, we can't say when, we can't say where—

Lord Krishna set an archer on the square:
The archer, torqued in fury, back in play,
Twisted around to see what lay behind
The sightless mazes, unseen labyrinths
Awaiting him, as if no time had passed,
Where mirror-image towers turned to smoke
And ashes, slowly moving off—
                                and saw
The god of writers rushing to record
The names of each and every one who died,

Ashes impregnated with human souls
Who couldn't save each other or themselves
In never-ending wars compounded by
Oblivion. Mortal forgetfulness.
What was it Krishna told him, long ago,
Back when another, ancient war recurred:
Moments replacing moments only once,

My deeds of wondrous love I here reveal:
There are no slayers here, there are no slain.
The conquered and the conqueror are one.
All come to me, all are accounted for—

The hero-archer halted, hung his head,
His godly bow Gandiva drooping down,
And turned—

        beyond the boundaries of the squares
He saw Lord Krishna seated, playing chess,
Lord Krishna, who had cousins on both sides—
He saw the blue hand gesture toward the board:

All that could be done has now been done.
I am the same to all, Lord Krishna said.
To all beings, my love is ever one.

And here—mid-tale, mid-war, mid-labyrinth,
Mid-birth and -death, mid–once upon a time,
And midway through the names of all who died

In wars we can't say where, we can't say when,
Their stories broken off, the fragments fused
Mid-genealogy, mid-epitaph,
Annihilation gusting nearer; *here*—
Here the god of writers broke his pen.